Young Entrepreneurs

Inspiring Stories of Children Who Made a Difference

Krishna Bista

STAR SCHOLARS PRESS

Young Entrepreneurs

First Reader Series
ISBN: 978-1-957480-34-3
LCCN: 202393224

Library of Congress US Programs, Law, and Literature Division
Cataloging in Publication Program
101 Independence Avenue, S.E. Washington, DC 20540-4283

Printed in the United States of America
Typsett: GM Solutions

This book is designed for classroom use and can be used for educational purposes without additional permission. Its stories and images were carefully selected with input from individual scholars. As a non-profit publication, this book is limited in print and intended to inspire young learners to make a positive impact in their communities and beyond. This project is supported by the Entrepreneurship Research Award.

About the book

Young Entrepreneurs is a motivational book for young readers. It includes ten young innovators and their paths to success, personal growth, and exceptional talents. This book tells you how these young entrepreneurs have initiated change in their areas of interest, overcoming obstacles and demonstrating remarkable innovation. These stories may serve as an inspiration, showcasing the profound influence of youthful creativity and determination in diverse fields.

About Author

Krishna Bista teaches at Morgan State University in Maryland and writes about what it's like to be a college student and how students can have exciting experiences by studying in different countries. Dr. Bista has written many books and articles about student experiences.

Contents

Chapter 1

Raelynn Heath

A Young Jewelry Entrepreneur

Image from starlandnews.com

At the age of eight years, Raelynn Heath was an entrepreneur who was already making a big difference. She grew up in Raytown, Missouri, and her journey is filled with creativity, determination, and a big heart.

Raelynn's adventure began when she was just four years old. At that young age, she started making bracelets using plastic beads. As she grew older, she tried new materials like acrylic and bubblegum beads. She even got creative by using soda pop labels, chip bags, and old clothes to make her jewelry unique. She mixes old and new things to create beautiful jewelry.

What makes Raelynn truly special is her kindness. She doesn't just make jewelry for fun; she also donates it to people in her community who are going through tough times, such as losing someone they love. She wants to make them feel better and bring some happiness into their lives. Her generosity is as impressive as her jewelry-making skills.

She uses social media sites such as Facebook and Etsy to show and sell her jewelry. Her hard work paid off when she was featured in a special showcase called the 1 Million Cups Black Entrepreneurship Showcase. This means lots of people noticed her amazing work. Because of her success, her mom is even getting a special license to make their jewelry business official. Her mom leads a group called G.I.R.L.Y (Gifted, Intelligent, Respectful, Leaders, and Young), which is all about helping young girls follow their dreams and become entrepreneurs, just like Raelynn.

Raelynn's future looks bright. She wants to keep growing her jewelry business and expand into other areas of fashion. One day, she dreams of owning a shop in a faraway place called Paris. But she also knows that school is essential, so she plans to attend college and learn more about fashion. With her determination and optimism, there's no doubt that she'll achieve her dreams.

Questions

1. Where does Raelynn come from?

2. What materials did Raelynn start using to make jewelry at 4?

3. How does Raelynn use social media to show and sell her jewelry?

4. What special thing does Raelynn do with her jewelry for people in her community?

5. What is Raelynn's dream for her jewelry business, and what does she want to do in Paris?

Chapter 2

Maya Penn

An Artist and Eco-Friendly Entrepreneur

Image from mayasideas.com

Maya Penn is a talented artist, a creative designer, and the boss of her own eco-friendly fashion company called Maya's Ideas.

Maya was born in Atlanta, and her journey as a young entrepreneur began at eight years old. Yep, she decided to start her very own business. She made beautiful things, such as accessories and clothes, and she made them with her own hands.

Now, you might be wondering, what does "eco-friendly" mean? Well, Maya learned that some clothes and things we use are not very nice to our planet Earth. They can be harmful and cause lots of pollution. So, she wanted her products to be friendly to the Earth and not hurt it.

Maya's Ideas became popular, and people from many countries, including Denmark, Italy, Australia, and Canada, started to buy her unique creations. But guess what? Maya isn't just about making money. She also donates 10-20% of the money she makes to help charities and groups that care for the environment.

Maya is also a super-talented artist and animator. She's been drawing since she could hold a crayon, and she started making flip books when she was just three years old! Animation is her big passion, and she even created a fun animated series called "The Pollinators" to teach people about bees and other insects.

Maya's story is quite a magical adventure that shows us how even young kids like you can make a big difference in the world.

Questions:

1. What is Maya Penn's business called?
2. Why did Maya want her business to be eco-friendly?

3. What does Maya do with some of the money she makes from her business?

4. What does Maya want to inspire other girls to do?

Chapter 3

Mikaila Ulmer

Me & The Bees Lemonade Entrepreneur

Image from bbc.com

Mikaila Ulmer is a young entrepreneur, and her story is like a lemonade recipe – sweet, inspiring, and full of surprises!

Mikaila was born in Houston, Texas. When Mikaila was just five years old, she decided to set up a lemonade stand right in front of her house. But this wasn't just any lemonade – it was her great-grandmother's special recipe from the 1940s. She added honey from local beekeepers and even some healthy flaxseed. People loved it!

Mikaila wasn't just selling lemonade for fun. She wanted to help save the bees. Bees are like nature's gardeners; they help plants grow by pollinating them. So, Mikaila decided to donate 10% of the money she made from selling lemonade to groups that protect bees. What a sweet idea!

As time went on, Mikaila's lemonade business grew bigger and bigger. It was like a lemonade explosion! She even appeared on a TV show called "Shark Tank" and got $60,000 to help her business grow. Imagine that!

Mikaila's lemonade journey didn't stop there. She met President Barack Obama at the White House, where he called her "an amazing young lady." In 2017, her lemonade, known as "Me & The Bees Lemonade," was sold in 500 American shops, selling 500,000 bottles each year. That's a whole lot of lemonade!

By 2020, her lemonade was in over 1,500 stores across the United States of America, including fancy places like Whole Foods. Mikaila's lemonade adventure was like a lemonade rollercoaster, full of ups and downs and thrilling surprises!

Questions

1. Where was Mikaila Ulmer born?
2. What inspired Mikaila's special

lemonade recipe?

3. Why did Mikaila decide to donate a portion of her lemonade profits?

4. What happened to Mikaila on the TV show "Shark Tank"?

Chapter 4

Riya Karumanchi

An Entrepreneur Who Invented Smart Cane

Image from stheamandapope.com

This is an inspiring story about Riya Karumanchi, a young entrepreneur. She's on a mission to make life better for people who can't see well, and she's doing it with a fantastic invention called Smart Cane. She was just 15 years old by then!

While visiting her friend's house, Riya met her friend's grandma, who couldn't see very well.

She noticed that the grandma had a white cane, but it wasn't helping her much. The cane was great for things on the ground but not so good for stuff higher up, like tables and chairs.

This got Riya thinking. She wondered why the white cane couldn't do more to help people. So, she decided to create a super-duper, high-tech version of the white cane.

Guess what? Riya's Smart Cane is like no other cane you've seen. It has GPS, just like the maps on your phone. It can give you directions by vibrating. If you need to turn left, it vibrates once, and if it's a right turn, it vibrates twice. How awesome is that? Smart Cane also has a special sensor that can tell you if there's something in your way, even if it's higher than your knees. So, you won't bump into tables or chairs anymore.

Riya isn't stopping there. She dreams of adding a smart camera to Smart Cane. This camera will be like your eyes, telling you what's around you. It can even recognize people's faces. Riya wants to make sure people who can't see well can do things just like everyone else.

Riya's hard work paid off as she secured funding for Smart Cane with an investment from Microsoft. She also leads a team of people, including engineers and advisors. Her innovative idea has been well-received by organizations like CNIB, Canada's organization for people with vision impairments.

Later, Riya attended Standford University for computer studies and continued other innovations. Her story shows us that no matter how old you are, you can make a big difference if you dream big and work hard. So, keep dreaming!

Questions

1. What inspired Riya to create Smart Cane?
2. How does Smart Cane help people get around better?
3. What's the job of the vibrating in Smart Cane?
4. Who's helping Riya with her fantastic invention?

Chapter 5

Lily Adeleye

The Youngest Entrepreneur

Image from women's wear daily

Lily Adeleye became the CEO of her own company called *Lily Frilly* at the age of seven years. Her company develops beautiful hair accessories like bows and barrettes. Lily's creations are available at Walmart, one of the world's largest retail stores. Lily Frilly products at Walmart now include Candy Rush Bow, Galaxy Girl Bow, Gold and Glitter Bow, Safari Party Bow, Confetti Fruit Clips, and others.

Lily's story teaches us an important lesson: you don't have to wait until you're all grown up to become an entrepreneur. Lily believes kids can achieve big dreams too, and she's here to prove it. Her hair accessories are not just pretty; they carry a message of inspiration for all the little girls out there.

Lily's success shows that if you have great ideas, work hard, and believe in yourself, you can accomplish amazing things. Her mom, Courtney Adeleye, is incredibly proud of Lily's creativity and determination. She knows that Lily has all it takes to be successful.

Questions

1. How does Lily inspire kids through her brand, Lily Frilly?
2. What message do Lily accessories carry for young dreamers?

3. How does Lily's partnership with Walmart demonstrate her success?

4. What can you learn from Lily's story about pursuing your dreams?

Chapter 6

Ryan Kaji

The Highest Paid Digital Entrepreneur

Image from time.com

Ryan Kaji was born in Houston, Texas. He has a YouTube channel with 35 million subscribers! That's like filling up a stadium, but not just once – over and over again. People have watched his videos more than 55 billion times! That's more views than the number of grains of sand on a beach. Is it mind-boggling numbers?

Ryan isn't just any regular kid; he has been the highest-paid YouTube star, with $30 million annually. Can you believe a child has such a mighty influence online? Some people call Ryan "the crown prince of YouTube."

He started his YouTube journey when he was just three and a half years old. He asked his mom if he could be on YouTube like other kids. Both his mom and dad helped Ryan follow his dreams. They even changed their family name to Kaji to keep their privacy as they became famous.

Did you know that Ryan and his parents have created something incredible? They've put Ryan's name on a whopping 1,600 different products in 30 different countries, including

Skechers shoes, cozy pajamas, exciting Roblox items, super-soft bedding, stylish watches, sporting goods, colorful water bottles, cozy furniture, refreshing toothpaste, and, of course, awesome toys! It's like having a piece of Ryan's world wherever you go.

Ryan's journey teaches us that dreams can soar no matter how young you are. With hard work and belief in himself, he turned his dreams into reality.

Questions:

1. How many subscribers does Ryan have on his YouTube channel?
2. How many views have people watched on Ryan's videos?
3. What valuable lesson can we learn from Ryan's journey?

4. What are some of the products that have Ryan's name on them?

5. Why is Ryan's story so remarkable, despite his young age?

Chapter 7

Oliver Frequiere

A Young Bath Bomb Entrepreneur

Image from shopify.com

Oliver "Ollie" Frequiere is from Brooklyn, New York. Ollie became the CEO of his business, "Fizzies & Fables," when he was six years old. It was all about making bath time an adventure. Ollie loved taking baths, and he wanted to share that joy with other kids. So, he came up with the idea of making bath bombs.

But these were not ordinary bath bombs. They were magical fizzies filled with surprises. Each one had a different scent and a hidden toy inside. Can you imagine the excitement of watching your bath bomb fizz and change colors in the water, revealing a surprise toy?

What made Ollie's bath bombs even more special was that he played a big part in creating them. He didn't just sit back and let others do the work. Ollie decided what colors the bath bombs should be, what scents they should have, and even their shape. It was like being a scientist and an artist all at once.

Ollie's favorite bath bombs were the ones with themes from Minecraft and Pokémon. These were his creations, and he was proud of them. Ollie shared his bath bombs with his friends, and they loved them too. He even gave one as a birthday gift to a friend who had an animal-themed party, and it was a big hit.

One of the best things about having his own business, according to Ollie, was the money. He saved up a lot of money in his piggy bank, and that made him feel proud and accomplished.

Ollie's story is an inspiring one. It reminds us that even at a young age, we can dream big and make those dreams come true. Ollie followed his passion for bath time and turned it into a creative and successful business. Who knows what amazing things you can achieve when you follow your own unique passions and dreams? Never stop dreaming, and never stop believing in yourself.

Questions:

1. What is unique about Ollie's business, Fizzies & Fables?

2. What is Ollie's favorite part of running his business?

3. How do Ollie's bath bombs change when they are placed in water?

4. What superhero character does Ollie love, and why does he feel a connection to that character?

Chapter 8

Jahkil Jackson

A Young Entrepreneur of Chicago

Image from shopify.com

Jahkil Jackson is a social entrepreneur with an extraordinary mission in life - to help others in need.

When Jahkil was eight years old, he went on a visit with his aunt and cousins to see homeless people living on the streets of Chicago. It was a heartbreaking sight. He couldn't bear to see people struggling and suffering in such difficult conditions, surrounded by rats and without basic necessities.

Jahkil knew he had to do something to make a difference. He wanted to give them all houses, but he soon realized that was a big challenge. So, with the help of his loving family, he came up with another idea - Blessing Bags. These were special bags filled with toiletry items such as soap, tissue, and socks, things that could help homeless people in their daily lives.

When he was eight, he started an organization called "Project I Am" to help homeless communities in Chicago and beyond. But that's not all! Jahkil also runs his very own clothing line called "Trophies." A portion of his money from selling clothes supports Project I Am. It's like his clothing line and his charity work are working together to make the world a better place. His work was featured on the "Young

Wonders: A CNN Heroes Special" program hosted by Anderson Cooper. This is a huge accomplishment!

One of Jahkil's remarkable talents is public speaking. He's so good at it that he was invited to be the event's keynote speaker. He has published books. Jahkil is just like any other kid who loves video games and basketball. He's proof that no matter how old you are, you can make a difference and inspire others to do the same.

Questions

1. What inspired Jahkil to start Project I Am?
2. What are Blessing Bags, and why are they important?
3. How can you make a positive impact in our community, just like Jahkil?

Chapter 9

Christon Jones

A Young Visionary Entrepreneur

Image from thetruthjones.com

Christon Jones, also known as "The Truth," Jones is an inspiring young entrepreneur. He is a skilled investor and founded his own financial education company, "Return On Investment."

Christon's story began at seven with a deep love for football. However, his journey on the football field was not easy. He faced tough challenges, including bullying from teammates.

He saw these challenges as opportunities to grow and become stronger.

With the support of his loving mother and his unwavering faith, Christon turned his struggles into a source of empowerment. He wrote a book called "The Win Within," sharing his experiences and insights on overcoming bullying in sports. By the age of eight, he had already sold over 500 copies, marking the beginning of an incredible journey.

At ten, Christon ventured into motivational speaking, sharing his inspiring story with people around the world. His message was clear and powerful: no matter your age or the challenges you face, you can achieve your dreams.

By thirteen, Christon was teaching others about stock investments and running his own company. His journey is a testament to the power of perseverance, creativity, and hard work in achieving one's goals. His story teaches us that success is not just about financial gains; it's about following your passions and making a positive impact.

So, let's set our goals high, work tirelessly, and believe in ourselves, just like Christon!

Questions:

1. Can you list two things Christon did when he was bullied?
2. In your own words, tell me why Christon wrote a book. What was it about?
3. If you were Christon and felt sad about something, what would you do to feel better?
4. How does Christon's story inspire you to approach your goals and challenges?

Chapter 10

Everette Taylor

A Young CEO and Entrepreneur

Image from everettetaylor.com

Everette Taylor was born in Richmond, Virginia. He faced some tough times during his childhood. He experienced homelessness while in high school, which meant he didn't have a place to live for a while. But he didn't let these challenges hold him back. He worked hard and attended Virginia Tech, a top university, to pursue his dreams.

At the age of 19, Everette started his first company. This company created special computer programs for events. His hard work paid off because, after just two years, he sold that company.

Later, he became the Vice President of Marketing at a company called Qualaroo. They developed software that helped people understand how others behaved online.

He also co-founded a community called GrowthHackers with his friend Sean Ellis. GrowthHackers is a club where people share secrets and strategies to make businesses grow. Imagine being part of a group where you can learn all the cool tricks to make a business successful!

In 2018, Everette founded his own company, ET Enterprises. Inside this big company, he had smaller companies such as PopSocial, MilliSense, ArtX, and more. PopSocial, one of these companies, became famous for its innovative use of social media to help other businesses. Everette's hard work and creativity earned him recognition in *Forbes* magazine!

Everette is an exceptional speaker too. He travels worldwide, sharing his life story and offering insights on entrepreneurship, technology, art, and mental health. People love listening to him because he's incredibly inspiring!

He became a brand ambassador for NASA, which is a significant achievement. NASA is known for its space and science innovations, and Everette helps spread the word about their exciting inventions and ideas.

In 2022, Everette became the CEO of Kickstarter, a famous platform where creative people, like artists and inventors, get support for their projects. As the CEO, he's making a big difference by helping these creative minds turn their ideas into reality. He's a role model for all of us, proving that anything is possible if you believe in yourself.

Questions

1. Where was Everette Taylor born?
2. What did Everette start when he was 19 years old?
3. What was the role of Qualaroo, the company Everette worked at?
4. What is Everette Taylor's current role as CEO?

Resources

Stories and facts about these extraordinary kidpreneurs who made incredible adventures in business were collected from a range of sources, including newspapers, TV shows, and books. Here is a list of key internet sources for additional stories of these young individuals.

Raelynn Heath
https://www.startlandnews.com/2018/04/raelynn-heath-raes-materials/
https://www.opengrowth.com/resources/journey-of-raelynn-heath-beautiful-and-bling

Maya Penn
https://mayasideas.com/book-1
https://www.huffpost.com/entry/maya-penn-fashion-designs_n_1263114
https://www.onebillionrising.org/638/div-spark-a-movement-through-the-creative-spirit/

Mikaila Ulmer
https://www.bbc.com/news/business-44860428
https://en.wikipedia.org/wiki/Mikaila_Ulmer

Riya Karumanchi
https://theamandapope.wordpress.com/2017/08/07/startup-14-year-old
https://www.cbc.ca/news/canada/toronto/smart-cane-company-1.4806713
https://hhhamilton.ca/Success-Stories-Riya-Karumanchi-s-SmartCane.html

Lily Adeleye
https://www.lilyfrilly.com/pages/about
https://wwd.com/feature/youngest-ceo-of-a-black-owned-business-lands-at-walmart-1234813471/

Oliver Frequiere
https://blavity.com/this-new-york-city-kid-hasnt-even-started-first-grade
https://www.becauseofthemwecan.com/blogs/culture/meet-the-six-year-old-ceo-of-a-booming-bath-bomb-business
https://yen.com.gh/150767-oliver-fequiere-meet-6-year-ceo-a-booming-bath-bomb-business.html

Ryan Kaji
https://time.com/6116624/ryan-kaji-youtube/
https://www.theverge.com/2020/11/19/21575169/youtube-ryan-world-amazon-show-animated-nickelodeon-ott-strea

Jahkil Jackson
https://jahkil.com/ https://www.cnn.com/2019/12/06/world/cnn-heroes-young
https://www.shopify.com/blog/kid-entrepreneur-jahkil-jackson

Christon Jones
https://www.thetruthjones.com/about
https://www.cnbc.com/amp/2022/06/19/black-business-owners-under-the-age-of-20-on-early-success-lessons.html

Everette Taylor
https://en.wikipedia.org/wiki/Everette_Taylor
https://breakingintostartups.com/everette-taylor-marketing-officer-skurt/ https://everettetaylor.com/bio

Related Books

Bayen, B. (2022). *Black trailblazers: 30 courageous visionaries who broke boundaries, made a difference and paved the way*. Hollan Publishing.

Briggs, S. C. (2022). *She led the way: Stories of Black women who changed history*. Revell.

Harriton, J., & Vu, M. (eds) (2022). *Good night stories for rebel girls: 100 inspiring young changemakers*. Rebel Girls, Inc.

Norwood, A. (2021). *Black heroes: 51 inspiring people from ancient Africa to modern day USA*. Rockridge Press.

Can you think of

someone who inspires you and why do they inspire you?

Inspiring Story

Which story in the book did you find most inspiring and why?

Also by the author

Thank You Notes

This book is like a garden that grew from seeds of ideas into a beautiful story, thanks to the help and love from many special people.

First, a big thank you to the Entrepreneurship Research Award for giving us the "water and sunlight" to help our garden grow. This means they supported making our book!

I also used something super cool technology called ChatGPT to help think of fun ideas, make our stories better, and make sure everything in the book was easy to read and super interesting. It's like having a robot friend who's really good at generating ideas and helping you write the stories.

A huge shout-out to Professor Mary Foster from Morgan State University for being an amazing guide and helping us make sure our book was the best it could be.

To my student friend, Schnell Reed Garrett who suggested several stories included in this book, and our book-making team: You guys are awesome! Chinwe Ihoma, Patricia Timmons, Rajendra Bista, Tina Pandey, Dr. Uttam Gaulee, Dr. Roy Y. Chan, Dr. Bo Zhang, Dr. Sahar Aghasafari, Dr. Franca Nwankwo, and Dr. Sharif Uddin – you all helped so much, and this book wouldn't be here without you.

Thank you to everyone for putting your hearts and brains into this book. Because of you, we can share these fun and inspiring stories with kids everywhere. Let's keep dreaming big and making cool things happen together!

Thank you, thank you, thank you!

Made in the USA
Monee, IL
04 November 2026

67376108R00030